David A. Hinton is a Reader in the Department of Archaeology at the University of Southampton. He teaches and researches the period from AD 400 to 1500, which is summarised in his book, *Archaeology, Economy and Society*.

He first excavated in Wareham in 1974, and since 1991 has been co-ordinating a research programme on Purbeck with a colleague.

He is a member of the Dorset Archaeological Committee, and edits its leaflet series, 'The Making of Dorset'. He is also a member of the Dorset Natural History and Archaeological Society, in whose invaluable annual *Proceedings* he has published several articles.

Following page
A grave in the seventh-eighth century cemetery at Ulwell, near Swanage. The skeleton is that of a man, who was between 35 and 45 years old when he died. His grave was lined with thin slabs of limestone, forming a cist. The feet and lower part of the legs had been destroyed before excavation, so his height cannot be estimated, but his bones show that he was healthy, and he had a good set of teeth.

SAXONS AND VIKINGS

DAVID A. HINTON

THE DOVECOTE PRESS

Two silver pennies minted at Wareham for King Ethelred
the Unready and shown at twice actual size. They date to
about 991-97, a time when huge quantities were minted to
pay the 'Danegeld'.

First published in 1998 by The Dovecote Press Ltd
Stanbridge, Wimborne, Dorset BH21 4JD

ISBN 1 874336 50 4

Series designed by Humphrey Stone

Typeset in Sabon by The Typesetting Bureau
Wimborne, Dorset
Printed and bound by Baskerville Press, Salisbury, Wiltshire

A CIP catalogue record for this book is available
from the British Library

3 5 7 9 8 6 4 2

CONTENTS

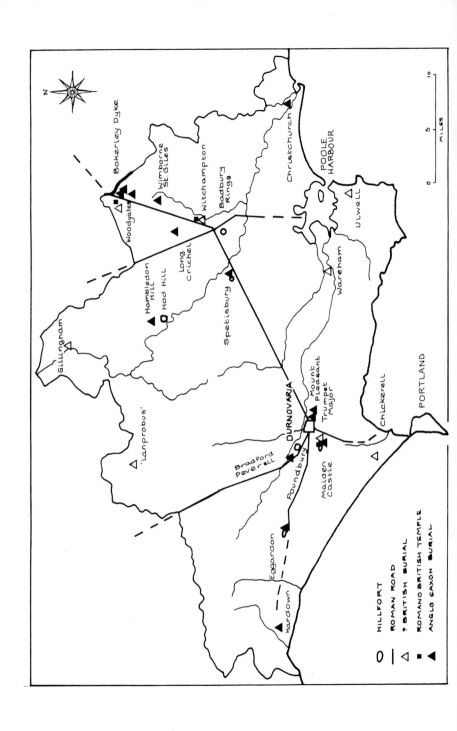

A REVOLUTION IN LIFESTYLES

'Happy is the country that has no history', because historical records are all about wars, famines and other events that bring disaster and misery. By that standard, the people who lived in Dorset during the two centuries after the end of Roman Britain in AD 409-11 should have been in a paradise, for no written texts describe what happened in the shire ('county' only after the Norman invasion), and there is not much archaeological evidence.

In some ways, it is wrong to talk about 'the end of Roman Britain', since the withdrawal of the legions and the collapse of the economic system that sustained the Empire would not have meant that everything suddenly changed. Although often called the 'Dark Ages' because of the lack of sources and the end of Classical civilisation, the post-Roman period may not have been so bad to live in. Between the middle of the fourth and the middle of the fifth centuries, the Britons certainly had to adapt to new circumstances, but may not have been fully aware of why, or even how, they were doing so.

Two great changes make interpretation of the fifth century particularly difficult, as both affect the amount of archaeological information available. Throughout Britain the use of coinage died away; no new coins were minted in the province, and new supplies were not regularly imported after AD 402 – there are a few later coins, but they are nearly all higher-value ones, some perhaps brought in to pay the remaining troops or to enable the Britons to pay their taxes, others to be used as easily-stored bullion. The way in which coins became less and less common has been shown by a study of those found on various sites excavated on Purbeck; after about

Map of Dorset showing the Iron Age hillforts that have some evidence of post-Roman use, the metalled Roman roads, and the sites of the British and 'Anglo-Saxon' burials mentioned in the text.

350 they disappear from farmsteads, then from villas, and finally from trading and industrial setttlements. After 402, they are occasionally found in hoards, but there were not enough low-value coins in circulation to use in everyday buying and selling.

The other great change was the end of the mass production of pottery, Dorset being particularly affected by the disappearance from the heathlands of the black-burnished ware industry. If manufacture had continued after money had gone out of use, new shapes of pot or new types of decoration would be found. Instead, there are only a few sherds in a coarser fabric than the older types, which may show how the industry was deteriorating; some pottery could have been made in the early fifth century, but the dating is not certain. Contacts between potters and customers could not have been maintained for very long without markets where pottery could be sold, and without the Roman army there was no state demand for bowls and cups for military tables and kitchens.

Because so little pottery was used in post-Roman Dorset, archaeologists cannot locate new sites by picking up sherds from the surfaces of newly-ploughed fields. Another problem is that people were not using stone and mortar, and other building materials leave much less trace of themselves in the ground – wood gets burnt or simply rots away, thatch roofs and daub walls that are left to collapse will soon revert to soil. These materials do not make the sort of marks in growing crops that air photographs can usually reveal, either. Often it is only when topsoil is stripped in advance of road-building or other development that archaeologists can identify where timber posts and beams were set in the ground; then, the holes dug to hold them can still be seen, if they have filled with material that contrasts to the subsoil around them.

A few late Roman villas may have stayed in use after their masonry walls had fallen into disrepair, but by people with a very different lifestyle from their predecessors'. Typical is the evidence from the Halstock villa in north-west Dorset, where a crudely made sherd of pottery and a few post-holes may post-date the fourth century, but are not enough to show whether anyone was living there, using it as a barn, or what.

Over time, most of the Romano-British farms and hamlets also

A Romano-British barn and grain-drier excavated at Worth Matravers. The abandonment of this building shows that the agricultural system was changing, with less emphasis on cereals. At the far end, the floor slabs were removed and a burial was inserted, which in turn was partly destroyed when someone dug a pit through it. Whether these events took place before or after the withdrawal of the Roman legions is unknown.

seem to have been abandoned, as people moved away to live at new sites. A recent excavation at Worth Matravers showed how frustratingly difficult it is to chart the process of abandonment and shift. There, a late Roman barn with a large grain-drier built into it did not simply collapse; instead, the drier was deliberately cobbled over to level it off with the rest of the building – perhaps an indication that the farmers using the drier were no longer under pressure to grow cereals intensively, but wanted a hard-standing for animals. The barn

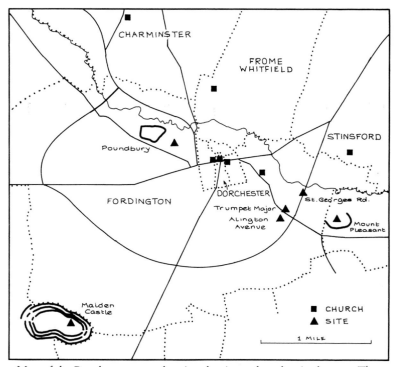

Map of the Dorchester area, showing the sites referred to in the text. The dotted lines are the parish boundaries, as recorded in the early nineteenth century – Fordington parish was very large, almost surrounding Dorchester. By the thirteenth century, and probably much earlier, there were three intramural churches, each with a small parish, perhaps carved out of Fordington's original jurisdiction. Charminster is Domesday Book's *Cerminstre*, 'the minster on the (River) Cerne'; its name suggests superior status. The roads include the modern by-pass, several others follow the lines of Roman roads, such as that south to the coast.

was probably already in a state of collapse when a single burial was inserted at one end. This grave was unmarked and soon forgotten, as a pit was dug that cut away the whole of the upper half of the body. The sequence of events is clear enough – but none of them can be dated, as the only objects in the features were amorphous fourth century pottery sherds.

In Dorchester (*Durnovaria*), excavations have shown how the infrastructure of public buildings, paved streets, water supplies and drainage was not maintained, and how owners of private houses could no longer enjoy hot baths or admire the mosaics on their floors. In the central part of the town, a courtyard house built in the second half of the fourth century was later sub-divided; a room in it that had originally had a mosaic was refloored with limestone flags; further change is shown by shallow slots that perhaps supported a timber fence butted up to an earlier wall to form an open yard; and the final use is shown by a few pieces of broken pottery that might have been made after about 400, including a sherd from an amphora that had come from (modern) western Turkey – brought by one of the last merchants from the Mediterranean to trade with Roman Dorset?

Elsewhere within Dorchester is a similar record of change rather than of sudden collapse. In the north-west corner, quite a grand town-house went out of use, its site used for grain-driers, for timber buildings interpreted as barns, and for activities such as blacksmithing. Perhaps grain was stored there, and turned into flour or malt before it was taken to market, or to the port near modern Weymouth to be shipped out to feed the Roman army. The owner of that property could have had another house in Dorchester where for a time he maintained a Romanised town lifestyle, but the overall picture is of changing standards well before the beginning of the fifth century.

An unmortared stone wall in the north-west corner might show some sort of enclave still in Dorchester long after the pottery and coin record dries up, but it has none of the sort of evidence excavated at Poundbury, on the site of a Roman extra-mural cemetery north-west of the town. Slots and holes showed that at various times some fifteen timber structures stood there, several on top of Roman burials. Some distinctive 'sunken-featured' buildings had involved digging a shallow, rectangular pit. There were grain-driers, blacksmithing evidence, and loomweights used in weaving. A few objects, such as combs, are similar in type to some found outside Dorset that are definitely post-Roman, and fifth and sixth century dates were obtained from radio-carbon.

Poundbury is the only large excavation of a Dorset site that certainly dates from immediately after the Roman period. There is

A reconstruction of a 'sunken-featured' building of the sort found at Poundbury. The walls were made of daub or clay, and the roof was thatched – materials that would leave almost no trace if left to rot on the site after the building went out of use.

smaller-scale evidence from St George's Road, Dorchester, where a 'sunken-featured' building could be contemporary with Poundbury's. That site was used in the fourth century, and probably like many others was not abandoned until well into the fifth or even later. There is a bigger site on the outskirts of Dorchester at Alington Avenue, which seems to be a little later, perhaps seventh/eighth century. There, too, there was late Roman settlement, but then perhaps with an interlude before people moved back onto it. There must be many other rural sites to be found in Dorset; those around Dorchester have been traced because most twentieth-century development has happened there – except in the south-east heathlands around Poole Harbour, where medieval occupation was probably always sparse.

LORDS AND FARMERS

How many people lived in Dorset in the fifth and sixth centuries cannot be reliably estimated, though it was probably a lot fewer than at the height of the Romano-British period. The decline has many possible explanations. Plague can devastate societies, but there is no definite evidence of it in fifth century Britain. The Picts and Saxons who raided the East Coast were too far away to have had much immediate effect on western Britain, and the Irish would have been a threat to Somerset rather than to Dorset, whose people were thus for a time protected by geography from slaughter and slavery. Climate change is also an unlikely cause of problems, for the slight fall in temperature that may have occurred would have had a minimal effect on the mild lowlands of southern England. Rising sea-levels would particularly affect Poole Harbour, and might have made a few people move inland a little. A few may have deliberately chosen to leave Dorset; there were Britons abroad in the fifth century, whose rowdy behaviour annoyed a bishop, and some of the rich perhaps had overseas estates on which they chose to remain. Large-scale emigration is unlikely, however.

Less dramatic reasons may explain population decline; in uncertain times, people limit the number of children that they have, for instance by marrying late if they do not feel secure enough to bring up a family. The growth of peat in one stream valley near Dorchester implies that the flow of water was restricted, as no-one cleared channels of debris such as fallen trees. If that pattern of neglect is typical, it may show reduced pressure to farm intensively, because there were fewer mouths to feed. Woodland may have increased, and scrub would have spread over the south-east heathlands without the demand for fuel for the Roman industries, but an analysis of pollen trapped in a peat bog near Bere Regis indicated that grassland was maintained.

Without the demand for cereals from the Roman army, widespread changes to farming practices are likely. The deliberate filling-in of the drier at Worth Matravers suggests less grain being grown in the area, with much of the labour-intensive ploughland being given over to grazing. The Poundbury driers, however, show that enough grain was still produced in the Dorchester area to warrant processing facilities; labour-saving free-threshing bread wheat was favoured, rather than the varieties grown in the Roman period. In comparison to what is found in *Durnovaria*, more sheep bones were found than cattle and pig, so fewer people were needed to tend the stock and fewer oxen to pull the ploughs.

Changes like these would be one reason for Roman rural settlements to have been abandoned for new sites, if new agricultural regimes were more conveniently managed from a scatter of individual farms rather than from larger settlements with many labourers. At Alington Avenue, the whole complex may have been no more than a single farm-house and its out-buildings – if the land stripped for the modern redevelopment included the whole of the archaeological site. The absence of post-holes suggests that its eastern and western edges were found, and it probably went little further south, as the ground slopes away. To the north, the Roman road was only a few yards away, so there would not have been space for many more structures – but were there other farms on the opposite side of the road?

The farms were able to feed people adequately. The bones of skeletons in a cemetery at Ulwell, near Swanage, were quite robust and well grown (see frontispiece), with no signs of malnutrition except for one or two cases of mild anaemia from iron deficiency. Soil conditions meant that many of the fifty-five skeletons were too badly preserved to be analysed, but nineteen women and fourteen men could be identified; there were also a few youths and children, but too few to be representative (high infant mortality can be assumed, but is usually difficult to prove because the bones survive less well, and the young may in any case not have been buried in the same places as adults). Six of the female skeletons could be measured, their heights varying from 1.50m (4′11½″) to 1.73m (5′8″). Only four males were measurable; they had much less of a range, from 1.69m

(5′6½″) to 1.73m (5′7″). Three of the women and four of the men died between the ages of 15 and 25, six women and only two men between 25 and 35. Seven women and seven men lived beyond 35, and some probably beyond 45, though the older the person, the more difficult it is to age their skeletons. Those who lived to 15 had a reasonable life-expectancy, though child-bearing put women at greater risk. Unsurprisingly, the older people became, the more they suffered from arthritis in their bones. Their work had been mostly manual, and quite heavy, but had not put intolerable strains on them; they were the sort of people whose lives had gone on despite political changes.

The withdrawal of the legions did not leave a power vacuum. The civilian magistrates who administered the Roman system probably developed new ways to control their localities during the last part of the fourth century, which helped them to hold onto power in the fifth. Without the cash income from their estates and their governmental offices, their resources were not enough for them to go on maintaining elaborate villas, but if they still owned estates, they could force their tenants to go on paying rents. Without coins, those rents had to be in kind, and landlords could insist on getting the best meat and ale on which to feast. They could coerce tenants into doing services for them, such as labouring on defensive works. They also continued to control the justice system, settling disputes and thus preventing violence. In societies that operate in this way, cohesion is given because everyone seems to gain; the people serve their lord, but in return he 'protects' them.

Something of this 'client' system may be recognisable at Poundbury. There were no economic reasons to make anyone want to suffer the physical difficulty of living in collapsing Dorchester once the market had gone and there were no fees to be earned from holding office. In the Poundbury cemetery still stood the impressive stone mausolea of the old elite; did their descendants go to live where their ancestors' shrines would remind everyone of their families' pre-eminence, which they were trying to maintain as their legal right? Overlooking Poundbury is an Iron Age hillfort, which a 'usurper' may have brought back into use, as the latest of the stone walls excavated along its rampart is not unlike the undoubtedly fifth/sixth century unmortared wall at South Cadbury, Somerset.

There were deer bones at Poundbury, suggesting that hunting rights gave the owner a supply of prestigious venison to offer at his feasts. The woods in which he hunted red deer may have been as far away as the Blackmoor Vale, if the Dorchester-periphery sites are showing that agriculture was maintained in the immediate region.

Sherds of imported pottery at South Cadbury and elsewhere in the south-west of Britain show that contact with the Mediterranean world was not completely lost. Dorset does not have tin and lead, metals which may have attracted an occasional merchant to visit British chiefs, bringing wine that they could serve to their most honoured guests. The only imported amphora sherds at Poundbury were like those found in Dorchester, and are probably late, not post-, Roman. The absence of imported sherds may be preventing recognition of some chiefs' seats.

Two glass beads of the sixth/seventh centuries found at Cleavel Point on Poole Harbour are similar to some found in eastern England, and in Francia (a large part of modern France), though where they were made is unknown. Whoever brought them had not come from the same part of the world as the merchants who took pottery to the rest of south-west Britain. One was found inside a timber building with a cobbled yard outside. No other post-Roman evidence was found there, and it may simply have been the house of a fisherman who made one or two longer journeys, returning with mementos. The beads may be evidence of trade, however, targeted at a local leader, whose residence might possibly have been on the castle hill at Corfe. This natural knoll was much altered in the later Middle Ages, but has some similarity to a post-Roman chieftain's stronghold in south Wales at Dinas Powys. The great ditch between Corfe's inner and outer baileys is reckoned to have had an earlier, shallower predecessor that extends beyond the bailey wall, and makes no obvious sense in relation to the stone castle; that ditch could be a lot earlier, therefore. At least one craftsman seems to have gone from

This aerial photograph of Corfe Castle shows clearly why the castle hill is always likely to have been important for anyone who wanted to control access from Purbeck to Poole Harbour. The church stands within an almost oval graveyard; this may just be because of the natural shape of the spur, but may be an indication of an early site.

The name of the Iron Age hillfort of Badbury Rings, seen here from the east, has led to many claims that it is the site of a battle where the British defeated the Saxons. The Roman roads that join at the crossroads to its south are clearly seen. Control of routeways would certainly have made it likely that the fort would be used, as it was in the early tenth century by King Edward the Elder, of Wessex.

Purbeck to Dinas Powys, since a Kimmeridge shale core and a flint for use on a lathe were excavated there. As there are no such finds in fourth century south Wales, these are not things that were taken up to the prince's residence from some earlier Roman site in the neighbourhood. A Dorset man may have heard a rumour about a distant patron, and gone to try his luck – which ran out if he tried to use Welsh coal when he had exhausted his stock of shale!

A different question is raised by two brooches, made no later than the middle of the fifth century, found on the slopes of Hod Hill, and a spear-head from within it. All are types that come from the Anglo-Saxon world to the east of Dorset. There is another spear-head from within the pre-Roman hillfort at Badbury. Were these the strongholds of British chieftains, to which they brought a few Saxons to boost their defences (Sturminster Newton castle, another natural knoll, has also been proposed)? Or are the objects residues of Anglo-Saxon attempts to advance into Dorset? Badbury is favoured by many as the location of the *Mons Badonicus* where the Britons had a victory, according to Gildas, a British scholar. Two recent writers have suggested that Gildas might have been working in Dorset, as he launches into long tirades against the behaviour of various kings in the south-west and Wales, but not against whoever ruled Somerset and Dorset. If Gildas was local, anything that happened at Badbury would have had great sigificance for him. But it is not even known when he was writing (opinions range from the second half of the fifth to the middle of the sixth century), so the Badbury spear-head cannot be fitted into a neat historical sequence.

Gildas calls British leaders of *Dumnonia* (Devon and Cornwall) and Wales 'kings' and Dorset may have been part of a sixth century kingdom based on the pre-Roman territory of the *Durotriges*, with the River Avon by then being a frontier zone with Anglo-Saxon kingdoms to the east. If that is correct, the Dorset chiefs were probably subservient to a more powerful lord or king who also ruled Somerset, which had greater resources. Most of the changes that were made to the great Bokerley Dyke bank and ditch complex in the north-east of Dorset on its Hampshire border probably belong to the politics of the period, with the old Roman road now called the Ackling Dyke being blocked to impede a Saxon advance. This is the road that went south-west past Badbury: was it used by a Saxon raiding-party that met its nemesis at *Mons Badonicus*, after which the British took steps to protect their frontier? The narrative may be tempting, but that does not make it true (and any temptation to write King Arthur into the story is best resisted). The earthworks do, however, show how chiefs could mobilise their people to do manual labour for what they saw as their country's need.

Wherever they were living, British lords would have tried to make sure that their estates survived as working units, and there are interesting arguments about whether this can be recognised. If Roman villas were estate centres, their lands would have remained as units even though the villas themselves were abandoned; so the boundaries of villa estates might have survived to re-emerge as medieval estate boundaries, such as those recorded in several tenth- and eleventh century charters (documents that record transfers of land from one owner to another), which often list the marker-points that defined an estate's boundaries. Although there may be no accurate, detailed maps until the 1830s and 1840s, drawn up to go with the tithe surveys, the nineteenth century parish boundaries shown on those are frequently recognised as being the same as those of the late Saxon estate boundaries, because the marker-points can be identified. Some parishes for which there are no charters may also therefore perpetuate late Saxon estates; had they been shaped by Roman estates?

The 'continuity' argument would look more convincing if in any one part of Dorset there were several parishes with a known villa in each. Furthermore, rather a lot of villa sites are quite close to parish boundaries, and it is unlikely that they would be on the edge of their own estates unless there was, for instance, a road running close to or along the boundary of their land, near which the owners needed to live. This does not seem to be the case; Roman roads are rarely followed by Saxon estate or parish boundary lines for more than short stretches, as the area around Dorchester illustrates.

What else may have survived? In a few cases, fields may have remained, but in general, when settlement sites changed, the arrangement of fields was probably changed too. Because people still needed

Bokerley Dyke, looking west. The foreground shows the massive bank, with a ditch on the Hampshire (right) side, mostly in shadow in this photograph. The straight line of another bank behind it is one of the many changes made to the complex, none of which is precisely dated; some or all may be post-Roman. In front of the belt of trees in the distance on the right is the Roman road, now known as Ackling Dyke; the long straight hedge-line shows its course southwards after passing the Dyke. The road was blocked by earthworks, preventing any traffic between Dorset's Badbury and Wiltshire's Sarum (Salisbury) – the latter being under different political control.

to communicate with each other, many lanes and tracks would have stayed in use, though new settlements might require new access routes as well as new fields. Anglo-Saxon charters often refer to 'herepaths' (=army routes) or 'highways', so there was an effective network. As for the paved Roman roads, they might survive if they were still needed, but the blocking of the Ackling Dyke in the north meant that it led nowhere, and became irrelevant – its name suggests that it came to be thought of as an old boundary, not a routeway. The road from Dorchester to Ilchester was probably more useful, linking the two parts of the Durotrigian territory. And when the 'Anglo-Saxon Chronicle' says that a king's reeve set out from Dorchester at the end of the eighth century to accost a party of strangers arriving at Portland by sea, he was probably riding along the old Roman road past Maiden Castle.

RELIGION – BURIALS

Christianity was known in fourth century Dorset, but it was not the only religion. The late Roman temple on the top of Maiden Castle has nothing Christian about its physical appearance; a round building was later added near-by and may be a post-Roman pagan shrine, as two such buildings in Somerset are thought to be. Four graves some yards away were aligned west-east as Christian burials usually were, but so too were many non-Christian ones. There may have been a temple at Witchampton, where what might have been post-Roman burials were recorded a long time ago. Similarly, burials in an enclosure near where there is thought to have been a temple or shrine at the west end of Bokerley Dyke could indicate continuing religious use.

In some fourth century graves in the cemetery at Fordington outside Dorchester, bodies were laid on their sides with their legs bent as though crouching, a practice which seems to have revived older, Durotrigian Iron Age traditions. Two graves at Poundbury which were dug through post-Roman features contained one crouched burial and one in which the legs had been drawn right up to the chin. One of those had even been buried with its head to the north, not the usual east, but as the remains were of a child, less need for normal procedures may have been felt.

Another Poundbury practice that might have been a revived Durotrigian one was lining the grave with thin stone slabs, and putting a stone cover over it, in effect creating a coffin. This idea may have come for Christian Gaul, however, where there are similar burials. Several were excavated at Ulwell (see frontispiece), where radio-carbon dates allow some of the burials to be as late as the eighth century, by which time Christianity was certainly practised. Two west-east examples were recently found outside Weymouth at Chickerell, their dates uncertain, but the absence of any grave goods

One of the post-Roman burials at Poundbury was of a child, who was placed in a roughly-cut grave dug mostly in the chalk, but partly in the dark filling of an earlier Roman gulley. The child's head is to the north, and its legs were pulled right up to its chest; the small foot bones can be seen. Its arms were also bent.

slightly favours the post-Roman period, and others elsewhere may have been misattributed to the Iron Age. Near Gillingham, a cemetery with at least a hundred burials is probably post-Roman, but few details were recorded when it was discovered in the last century.

If there was any awareness of Durotrigian burial practices, their appeal would have been to encourage people to bind together around their common ancestry against the outside world's threats. That would have been made stronger if it had gone hand-in-hand with revival of the older religions, a rejection of the new Christianity that had failed to hold the Empire intact. Overall, however, it seems likely that Christianity had already been adopted by most of the local aristocracy in fourth century Dorset, and their descendants continued to foster it so that their religion would imply that they were the inheritors of Roman authority and prestige. Certainly Gildas accused the Britons of many things, but active paganism was not one of them.

Evidence for beliefs about burial and society comes from five stones onto which Latin inscriptions have been cut, now kept in Lady St Mary Church, Wareham (see illustrations on following page). One was found built into part of the nave wall, reused as a piece of rubble, and it is likely that all five are not far to-day from where they were originally put up, a cemetery in which standing stones commemorated the most important occupants. Stones like these are found in Scotland, Wales, west Devon and Cornwall, and in Gaul, but nowhere to the east, and there are no others in Dorset. They have different styles of lettering, which implies different dates, though no-one agrees over what those dates are. One commemorates a man called Catgug, and looks quite like one in Gwynned set up for Cadfan, known from other sources, and datable therefore to the seventh century. Others at Wareham may be later than this, one a little earlier.

All the names on the Wareham stones are British except for Gideo, from the biblical Gideon, and most have the Latin word *filius*, 'son' – so it was important for those commemorated to record who their fathers had been. One of the names begins *Iud-*, Welsh for 'lord', and *Cat-* is the same as the Welsh *Cad-*, for 'battle', implying a warrior hierarchy claiming the right to rule from their fathers. All were cut into bits of Roman masonry, presumably brought from an abandoned

Above and opposite page Two of the memorial stones at Wareham. The one above has the name Catgug (with the A cut upside down). The one opposite is incomplete, but was probably Deniel. Both inscriptions then go on to give the names of the men's fathers. Catgug's stone was a reused Roman pillar, cut square to take the lettering. The other is cut onto a Roman shaft left with its original round surface.

villa, or down-river from Dorchester; Roman stonework was not used for any of the south-western inscriptions, and for only two in Wales, a milestone and an altar, not the architectural debris selected at Wareham, where not merely convenient flat surfaces were chosen, as some are round columns.

The Wareham stones strongly suggest that the people commemorated were aristocrats, but that does not mean that some or all were not priests as well. Inscriptions in Wales are both to rulers and to members of church communities. The possibility that the idea of erecting such stones came originally from Gaul is important, too, for it shows that Dorset Britons were still in contact with the other side of the Channel, even though there is no pottery or other material evidence for it. An origin there for the idea of slab-lining graves becomes more credible. When St Aldhelm was in Wareham in the early eighth century awaiting a boat for France, perhaps he was

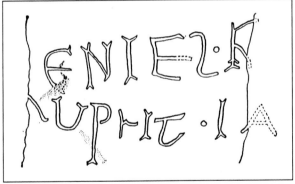

taking advantage of a regular and long-established crossing-point.

Before the end of the sixth century, there are a few burials in Dorset that are very different from those at Poundbury or Ulwell. A cemetery outside Christchurch contained several graves in which objects like spears and shields had been carefully placed. The burials were grouped around an old Bronze Age barrow, as though being used to bolster the claims to the local area of people who were able to show that they had taken control of its ancient sacred places. These customs came from the Anglo-Saxon world of Hampshire and

A view of the excavation of the Bargate cemetery outside Christchurch. The round feature is the ditch of a prehistoric burial mound; this barrow may have been visible when the area was chosen as a cemetery for people who buried their dead with objects, in the 'Anglo-Saxon' fashion. One of the excavated graves is the rectangle where the circle is incomplete.

Although spear-heads are common in graves, this one from Hardown Hill is exceptional in having a pattern punched into it, which looks as if it represented a fish. The open socket would have taken a long shaft, usually made of ash-wood, and held firm by the rivet, which can be seen near the end.

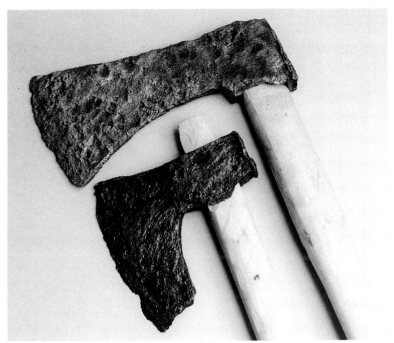

One of the most unusual objects from Hardown Hill was the head of an axe, the lower of the two shown here mounted on modern shafts. There are very few battle-axes in early graves, though they were certainly widely used later. The upper axe is a general-purpose tool, made in the fourteenth or fifteeenth century, and is shown for comparison.

Wiltshire, and the Christchurch cemetery may well be that of a Saxon enclave establishing itself around the lower Avon, the weapons in the graves emphasizing that these were people ready and able to defend themselves. A thin scatter of other finds from the area suggests that they held their own.

Spear-heads found in the last century at Spetisbury may indicate a cemetery there like that outside Christchurch, perhaps serving another colonising settlement – the number of spears seems too many for accidental loss, which may account for the earlier one at Badbury. There is a single grave with a sixth century brooch and a necklace at Wimborne St Giles – a Saxon lady married outside her kin? More extraordinary is the record from Hardown Hill, overlooking the coast right over in west Dorset. There, also in a barrow, were found during the First World War (and neither excavated nor recorded properly) Anglo-Saxon types of spear-head, a shield-boss, an axe-head and a brooch. Whether they were from a single grave or from a small cemetery is uncertain, but a mid sixth century date, earlier than the Christchurch dates, is possible. Does Hardown Hill represent a small community that failed to establish itself, or a single warrior whose luck ran out in a raid?

RELIGION – BRITISH CHURCHES

Unlike many Roman towns, such as Exeter, there is no trace inside Dorchester of a post-Roman church or cemetery. A small polygonal feature at Poundbury has been interpreted as a screen for an altar, because it can be compared to one at a site in Gloucestershire where there was a church, which at Poundbury could have been the function of a nearby rectangular building. There was also a ditch which perhaps enclosed the area round the complex, as though to separate it off from the rest of the world. A church at Poundbury may have been considered an appropriate extension to a chief's residence, adding spiritual to physical protection – a common focus for people to come to, to pay their respects to their god and their tribute to their lord. If a church had had long use, however, burials might have been expected around it, though not the unorthodox ones described in the previous chapter.

Aristocratic patronage offered communities of priests the support and supplies that they needed for themselves and their pupils, and servants to do the chores to give them time for their studies. Gildas, for instance, wrote in Latin – good Latin, so he was well-educated, and he expected other people in Britain to understand him. One such community was probably at Wareham, as the inscribed stones show that some people there could at least construct a simple Latin text.

By the end of the seventh century, information from charters dealing with land-ownership begins to be another source about churches, although nearly all of it survives because later writers copied it, not always accurately, from documents that have now vanished. One charter tells how an Abbot Bectun, a British name, was given 'thirty hides' at *funtemel* after about 670. 'Thirty hides' would have supported thirty families, or working farms – producing enough surplus to satisfy their lord's demands for payments in kind. *funtemel* may have been a large bloc of land west of the Roman road from Badbury,

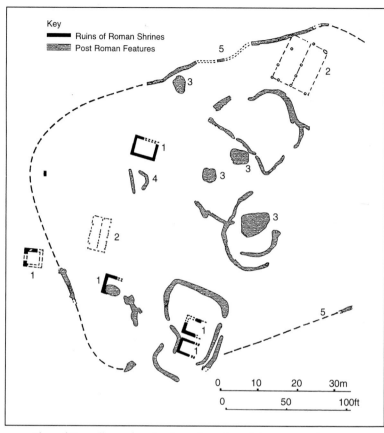

Plan of Poundbury showing how the ruins of the rectangular stone 'mausolea' of the Roman period (1) may still have been standing when the site was being used in the post-Roman period. It seems to have been enclosed by a ditch (5), and the timber buildings (2) may have included a church. The possible screen is the apsidal structure (4). There were also sunken-featured buildings (3) like the one illustrated on page 12.

represented by the present-day parishes of Fontmell Magna and Ashmore. It was later sold to a church at Tisbury (Wiltshire) which was subsequently owned by Shaftesbury Abbey, the nunnery founded in the late ninth century. Bectun's church might have been at Shaftesbury, though Iwerne Minster is closer to Fontmell and is another possible site, and it may not have been in Dorset at all.

As with Shaftesbury, a British predecessor of Sherborne Cathedral, centre of the see founded in about 705, is a possibility. There is an early reference to a *lanprobus*, and twelfth century records of a 'Propeschirche' and a chapel of St Probus, who is otherwise known only in Cornwall, a county in which 'lan' names are common, and are similar to the Welsh 'llan', used of many church sites. The twelfth century references place St Probus's Chapel at the later castle, outside Sherborne, where burials and a ditch have been excavated; as these pre-date the Norman work, it may well be here that *lanprobus* was situated. Its importance to Sherborne Cathedral seems to have been mainly that its estates were transferred to the new see, not that it had any significance as a predecessor on the site of what is now the abbey.

Another British church may be identifiable at Whitchurch Canonicorum. Its name simply means White-church, presumably because it was distinctive for being white-washed. As a *Hwitan-cyrican* in King Alfred's will is quite probably this Whitchurch, the name existed by the late ninth century. In the eleventh, it was *Witcerce* or in Latin *Album* (=white) *Monasterium*, and had been acquired by a Norman abbey; donations like that of once-important churches were quite common, Wareham being another. So there are hints that Whitchurch was more than just an ordinary church; but is it therefore British in origin? A clue is that at least by the twelfth century a cult of St Wita had developed at Whitchurch, where there is a late twelfth century Purbeck marble shrine. St Wita's name could have arisen because the original, descriptive meaning of the church's name had been forgotten, and a saint was created to 'explain' it. Alternatively, there had been a British church on the site, dedicated to a saint whose name became increasingly obscure, like Sherborne's Probus, until it slid into disuse and an alternative was adopted that seemed to explain the *wit* in the church's name. (The shrine remained popular, and visits by many medieval pilgrims made the church profitable, so it was acquired by the canons of Salisbury Cathedral: hence the 'Canonicorum' part of the modern name.)

Yet another possibility is that Whitchurch was originally known by the name of its owner and founder, a secular landlord; as all memory of him faded, it came to be assumed that he was a saint, for whom it

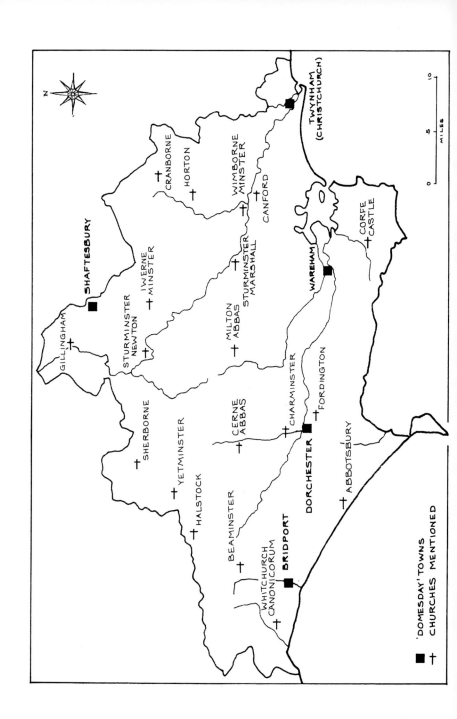

was logical to make a shrine. Most of Dorset's churches are dedicated to biblical saints, or to St George or other late cults, but some may have had earlier dedications which became so obscure that they were changed. There are too many possibilities for certainty.

Although the present church building at Whitchurch Canonicorum is twelfth century and later, large quantities of Roman brick are used in its walls, so presumably there was a Roman villa near-by. Some Roman villas could have become the sites of British churches. Mosaics like that at the Hinton St Mary villa show that the owner knew about Christianity; did such people have house-churches, and if they did, did they employ priests and expect their tenants to come there to worship? If so, the tradition of a church might have become strong enough for it to survive as an institution even after the villa that fostered it had gone. The absence of recognisably early Christian burials from villa sites is one reason for doubting the survival of churches at them, however. This is an argument that is linked to the problem of Roman estate boundaries surviving to become parish boundaries, since the church's interest in perpetuating the area over which it had spiritual dominion would be as great as the landlord's to perpetuate his income. The same objections apply; there are a few possible cases, but no known villa has been shown definitely to have had any significance for later church organisation. There is a big villa in Iwerne Minster parish, for instance, but it is a thousand yards from the present church – in a large parish in good farming land, perhaps the absence of a villa would take more explaining!

Other examples of claimed associations between Roman buildings and later churches include Sherborne and Wimborne Minster. In both, mortar floors have been reported, but they are more likely to be those of parts of the Saxon churches than of underlying Roman villas, and excavations at Sherborne found no evidence of a Roman structure around the church. Nor has anything Roman of consequence been found in Wimborne – there have been several excavations in the town, though none close to or in the church. Although there was Roman occupation in the area around Lady St Mary

Map showing the location of the churches discussed in the text of this book, and of the places treated as towns in Domesday Book.

[35]

Church at Wareham, no trace of a villa has been found there, the only Roman masonry being the pieces reused for the memorial stones.

Another debatable case is Tarrant Crawford church, because Roman tiles are said to have been found below its floor – but it is a small church with a small medieval parish, and no evidence that it was an early foundation. The Roman altar used as a footing for the chancel arch at Godmanstone was quite probably carted there the five miles from Dorchester, but in the twelfth century when redevelopment meant that people were digging into the underlying Roman strata. Halstock – 'Holy place' – looks significant; there was a villa in the parish, though again a long way from the church, and the place may have acquired the name merely because it was owned by Sherborne. In the ninth century, however, it was a royal estate of fifteen hides, given to a deacon, which suggests an independent church of some importance, and later tradition ascribed St Iudhael's relics to it.

The position of the large church in the middle of the Roman cemetery outside Dorchester at Fordington could possibly be explained by the survival there of a shrine at a Christian *mausoleum*, but that would be a very different form of continuity from that of a villa's house-church. If Poundbury was indeed for a time the site of a British church, it too might have orginated as a shrine at one of the *mausolea* there. Its disappearance without trace shows how easily such places could pass into oblivion. The disuse of the cemetery at Ulwell after the eighth century is another reminder that religious places did not always achieve long-term stability.

The name Ulwell first occurs in the thirteenth century as 'Holewell', which at first sight looks likely to be 'Holy well', but the meaning is actually 'well, spring or stream frequented by owls'. Nevertheless, it is a reminder that waterside locations are quite common for early churches and chapels, and that a church may have existed at a site long before the oldest part of its known building was begun. The difficulty is that in Dorset, there are not all that many places that are far from water in one shape or form.

Another Dorset church raises the very different question of whether any pagan temples or shrines were taken over by

The ruins of the chapel at Knowlton stand within a prehistoric bank with an internal ditch. Despite this ready-made enclosure, the building had an almost square yard around it, as the photograph clearly shows; a curved boundary is often a sign of an early church foundation.

Christianity, as Pope Gregory recommended. At Knowlton, a twelfth century church building inside a prehistoric bank and ditch looks at first glance as though it could be an example of precisely this practice. Gregory, however, was probably talking about taking over pagan buildings, not of building churches where it was thought that old religions had once been practised. If there were churches inside other prehistoric henges, or close to standing stone circles, a pattern could be recognised; but there is no comparable case in England of the former, and none in Dorset of the latter. Knowlton was not a parochial church in the Middle Ages, but a chapel; the present building could replace an earlier one, but there are many chapels, like St Catherine's at Abbotsbury, which were built in the later Middle Ages to be visible signs of Christianity in prominent places. Knowlton does not really fit that criterion, however. The local Hundred used to assemble at Knowlton, and there may have been a feeling that a chapel was needed to bless its deliberations. But in that case, why were other open-air meeting-places not provided for in the same way? Knowlton is puzzling, but it does not provide a model for any general rule about pagan conversions; 'hard cases make bad law'.

THE SAXON CONQUEST

Abbot Bectun's *funtemel* estate is recorded as being the gift of King Cenred, with adjacent land being owned by Leuthere, Bishop of Winchester, who died in about 676. If these names can be trusted, they show that north Dorset was by then ruled by the West Saxons, for Cenred was a king of the *Gewissae*, and Winchester was their diocese. A record that an earlier Saxon king, Cenwalh (642-72), had donated a large estate to Sherborne may have been written much later to associate an important king with the foundation of the church, instead of some less significant figure; nevertheless, Cenwalh's victory in 658 at a battle probably fought in east Somerset may well have given him control over at least the north part of Dorset. Although no narrative of the conquest can be constructed from the 'Anglo-Saxon Chronicle' and other documents, by 705, King Ine of Wessex was able to establish his sister in a nunnery at Wimborne, so he was confident of his hold over south-east Dorset by then, and in that year St Aldhelm and he seem to have been able to include the whole of the shire within the new Sherborne diocese.

Growing Saxon influence on seventh century Dorset is also shown by archaeological evidence, especially burials. Typical is a small group of two males and a child, inserted into the middle of a Bronze Age barrow on Launceston Down, Long Crichel. One of the men had been buried with a copper-alloy buckle and a sheathed knife at his waist, presumbly his belt-fittings, and an iron buckle and a tool. Burials with buckles and knives are common in the seventh century Anglo-Saxon world. Comparable burials include a group of twelve on Hambledon Hill, and others in the north-east towards Bokerley Dyke. The child's presence, and perhaps the woman at Wimborne St Giles, show that these are not the graves of Saxon warriors who died fighting their way southwards, but of more prosaic settlers, perhaps in family groups, whose burial customs were Anglo-Saxon. It is

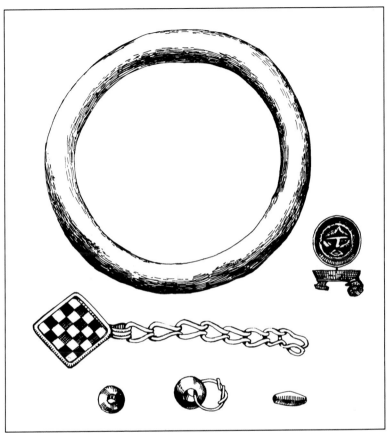

Drawing of some of the Anglo-Saxon grave-goods excavated in the early nineteenth century in north-east Dorset. All but the brooch (right) came from a barrow in Woodyates, in which a woman had probably been laid on an elaborate bed-like bier; the ivory ring (half actual size) was probably the top of a bag in which small treasures were kept: such rings seem generally to date to the second half of the seventh century. Below it is a gold panel containing glass of different colours, known as millefiori, with a gold chain, probably once part of a short necklace (twice actual size), and at the bottom are three beads, of jet, glass and gold (actual size). The brooch (actual size) is copper alloy, gilded to glint like gold, and shows a human face. This is a design that is found in the sixth century, mostly in southern England; it may have been quite old when it came to be buried in a barrow on Oakley Down (Wimborne St Giles), but the many beads found with it suggests a long necklace of the kind usually favoured in the sixth century.

Photograph taken during the excavations of Maiden Castle by Mortimer Wheeler in the 1930s, showing the male skeleton found near the temple. The two knives buried with him are lying across the upper part of his left leg, which suggests that he was wearing them in a scabbard hung from his belt.

usually assumed that they were migrants from Hampshire and Wiltshire, infiltrating under the protection of the *Gewissan* kings. It is just possible, however, that they were actually native British, adopting the customs of the Anglo-Saxons to conform to the practices of their new overlords.

A single seventh century burial near the temple on the top of Maiden Castle may have been located there to be prominent rather than because of any standing ruins or remembered sanctity. The grave contained a man with a small knife and a late seventh century single-edged sword, a weapon that seems to have been more ceremonial than functional, and is associated with the highest social ranks. He may well represent another element in the process by which the Anglo-Saxons achieved control over Dorset: a male warrior sent as a royal agent, a 'shire-reeve', his sword expressing his authority. There is another seventh century burial nearby, of someone apparently hacked to death, with savage cuts to his head and limbs. There may be no connection between the two burials, but the second one certainly shows the effectiveness of contemporary weapons.

Other burials may belong to the new seventh century pattern, but if they were interred without objects, as was increasingly the case

One of the most interesting objects from the seventh century cemetery at Bradford Peverell is made of copper alloy coated with white metal so that it would look like silver. At each end there is a dragon's head with a long snout turned up at the end, an eye, a crest on the top of the head (broken at the left end), and a shorter curling lower jaw which with the creature's curved neck forms a circle – into which rivets could have been inserted, to hold the oject in place. The three funnel-like projections on the bar may have held further decoration. The object may have been a fitting from a purse, but is unlike most of those that have been recognised, and use as a harness-mount is another possibility. Even the animal heads are unlike most of those that figure on objects or in manuscript paintings of the time.

among the Anglo-Saxons, they can only be dated by radio-carbon, which is not always possible. A small group at a barrow on Eggardon Hill is an example. Very different is a cemetery at Bradford Peverell, three miles from Dorchester, where some sixteen graves have been excavated. Several contained iron knives, some also buckles, one had a bone comb and a purse, and a girl had a necklace on which were hung a gold pendant, two silver discs, a gold bead, three glass beads and other objects. There was probably another rather similar cemetery at the 'Trumpet Major' just outside Dorchester on the Wareham road, though this was found in the 1850s, and little survives from it. Not far away at Mount Pleasant are two other probably seventh century graves. The Dorchester area clearly remained focal, even though the town itself was yet to be reoccupied.

The wealth and locations of these graves suggest aristocrats moving into the Dorset heartland, perhaps given estates in reward for their support of the West Saxon kings. They may have displaced some of the native landowners, but there may have been many cases of assimilation, with some Britons coming to terms with the new rulers. The *Gewissae* were Christian, and the nature of their rule, as 'kings' over petty kingdoms, was probably not very different from that of the Durotrigian kings whom they ousted. The Saxon King Ine's law-code makes provision for 'Welshmen', whose values were less than that of their English equivalents, but were nevertheless substantial. The names of the *Gewissan* kings suggest that there may have been mixing even in the royal family; Cenwalh's contains *walh*, the Old English for 'Welsh' or 'Briton' (and later, 'slave'), as though he was recognized as partly non-Saxon, and one of his successors, Caedwalla, had an entirely British name, including the *cat/cad* for 'battle' that occurs on one of the Wareham stones. All this suggests integration as well as conquest.

Integration may also be seen in the way that some aspects of people's material lives changed. The 'sunken-featured' buildings around Dorchester may be one example of willingness to adapt to new modes, as they are otherwise known only to the east of Dorset – yet they may pre-date the Saxon kings' conquest. The plans of the buildings at Alington Avenue seem different from the ground-level ones at Poundbury, being larger, with more substantial post-holes – and are also more like those at sites further east. Similarly, pottery that contains chopped-up grass and straw, probably because dung was mixed with the clay to help to bind it, used to be thought exclusively 'Anglo-Saxon', but has now been recognized at a few 'British' sites, including Poundbury – though the very little found in Dorset is not closely datable.

Sadly, the Christchurch cemetery was on a sandy site, and natural acid had completely eaten away the bones; although some could be seen as dark stains in the sand, they could not be measured, nor their sex identified, so that 'Saxons' there cannot be compared to 'Britons' at Ulwell. In a recently excavated cemetery in west Sussex, the average female height was 1.62m (5′3½″), male 1.74m (5′8½″). So five of the seven Ulwell 'British' women, and all the men, were shorter than the norm in one 'Saxon' cemetery. Very difficult to assess is the significance of the claim that blood-groups in

One of the post-Roman rectangular buildings excavated at Alington Avenue is clearly recognisable from the dark holes contrasting with the surrounding chalk, into which posts had been set. The holes seeem to be in double rows, which may mean that there was an outer line of buttresses along each side wall. The large areas of undisturbed chalk suggest that the settlement occupied quite a small space.

modern Dorset are different from those in Hampshire, and show Celtic genetic traits; such differences seem unlikely to have survived into the present day, as there has been so much population movement in the intervening 1,300 years, but it would certainly favour the argument that very few English people moved west into Dorset. Whatever happened to their landlords, the working farmers would have gone on with their daily round, as their production was no less important to the new than to the old estate owners.

One change that certainly occurred was in the language, for the indigenous Dorset folk must have spoken Celtic. Place-names sporadically recorded in charters, and more comprehensively in the late eleventh century 'Domesday Book', are mostly of English derivation, however. Surviving Celtic place-names are usually those of prominent landscape features, such as rivers and streams which have given names to estates and settlements alongside them: *funtemel*

(Fontmell), Tarrant (Crawford) and Iwerne (Minster) are examples. Other survivals include Creech, from *crug* (hill), and Lytchett (Matravers/Minster), from *led ced* (grey wood).

'Dorset' is from *Dornsaete*, meaning 'people of the Dorchester region'. *Dorn-* is from *Dornwaraceastre*, the name for Dorchester. The Romans called their city *Durnovaria* (or *Durnonovaria*), a word seemingly derived from Celtic: *-ceastre* derives from the Latin, *castra*, 'camp', and is a 'loan-word' (i.e. one borrowed from another language, in this case one learnt only by an educated minority) used for a time in Old English, mainly to refer to a Roman walled town or fort. *-saete* is Old English, akin to the modern 'settlers'. So three different languages were involved in creating 'Dorchester' and 'Dorset'.

Almost all the other places mentioned up to now in this book have no trace of Celtic in their names. Wareham is either the *ham* (homestead) or the *hamm* (meadow) by the *waer* (weir), all Old English words, though the church must once have had a British name. Badbury is the *byrig* (fortress) of *Badda* (a man's name) with no trace of the name *Vindocladia* recorded in the fourth century. Sherborne is *scire* (bright, clear) *burnan* (stream) – the generic word for 'stream' was English, even if a few individual Celtic stream-names were still used. Wimborne is the 'meadow stream', from *winn*. No British *lan* names are now to be found in Dorset, though *lanprobus* suggests that there were some once.

One of the earliest English names may be Witchampton, probably the *tun* (farm) at the *wicham*, derived from the Latin *vicus* (settlement) and Old English *ham*, a combination which may mean that incoming Saxons recognised it as a place which had a Roman origin, close to the Ackling Dyke road. If King Alfred's biographer is to be believed, Dorset was still referred to by the Welsh as *Durnguier*, implying that at least a few people remembered some earlier names in the late ninth century. On the other hand, although he mentions Wareham, he does not reveal its pre-English name, so presumably most of the changes had already taken place. Boundary marks named in charters are even better evidence, as they use almost exclusively Old English words for minor landscape features such as fields and trees. It is unlikely that Saxon landlords would have forced the use of

English words for such trivia upon farmers and peasants who used different words for them in their everyday lives. A few incomers do not usually change the whole structure of a language – English was not ousted by Norman French after 1066. Yet Devon and Shropshire have as little archaeological evidence of Anglo-Saxons as has Dorset, and there too most Celtic names have been lost to English. The reasons behind the disappearance of the British language are not really understood.

Many villages and most farms have names using Old English words, like *tun* and *worth*, often with an owner's name, as in Godmanstone, 'farm belonging to a man called Godmann'. When an owner died, the new owner's name would often be substituted, as in Afflington, *Alvronetone,* named after Aelfrun, a woman with an estate there in 1066. She was not its founder, but her name stuck because it became formalised by its use in 'Domesday', after which changes of name became less frequent. Another reason that so many places have no trace of Celtic in their names is because the *tuns* and *worths* were on new sites, first occupied after about 700, as shifting settlement patterns left many old ones abandoned and forgotten, like those around Dorchester.

SOCIAL AND ECONOMIC CHANGE

The name *lanprobus* only survives because of Sherborne's claim to its 100-hide estate, which implies that there were some very large land units in seventh century Dorset, even bigger than Abbot Bectun's thirty hides at *funtemel*. The supposed transfer is also important for suggesting how the Wessex kings could reorganize their newly-acquired territory, in this case suppressing a British church in the interests of the new bishop. Attempts to reconstruct the original land area of the hundred hides, from parish and charter boundaries, have led to different interpretations, but 'Domesday Book' has the Sherborne area as the most densely populated in Dorset, so it was probably already well stocked with farms in the seventh century.

The other major new church was King Ine's foundation at Wimborne, a 'double house' with two monasteries, one for men and one for women, but both ruled by Abbess Cuthburh, Ine's sister; the idea of 'princess-minsters' like these came from Francia. Unfortunately there is no record of the land endowment, but it must have been substantial if the king's sister was to be supported in appropriate style. Although nothing of the first church buildings survives, there is a graphic account of how the two monasteries were 'surrounded with high and stout walls', the only people allowed to go from one to the other being priests to say Mass in the nuns' church. Even visiting bishops were not allowed to enter the women's enclosure, Cuthburh talking to them through 'a little hatch'. Wimborne was highly regarded internationally, one of its nuns becoming abbess of a church in Germany.

Alfred's biographer says that there was a nunnery at Wareham by the ninth century, and the 'Anglo-Saxon Chronicle' records that King Brihtric was buried there in 802, which almost certainly means that it had royal patronage. Just as *lanprobus* may have been dissolved for the benefit of Sherborne, so probably was the British church at

This nineteenth century watercolour of Lady St Mary Church, Wareham, is one of the few records of what the Anglo-Saxon parts looked like. The nave, east of the tower, was tall (the battlements were added later), with round-headed windows, and had a two-storey *porticus* half-way along, with a distinctive arch made from large irregularly cut stone blocks. The arch was not open, but contained a blank wall, in which was set a square carved panel, now kept inside the church, and below it a triangular-headed door.

Wareham attested by the memorial stones replaced by the nunnery. Perhaps Bishop Aldhelm was responsible; certainly his twelfth century biographer says that he stayed in Wareham and founded a church at Corfe. Only the tower survived nineteenth century rebuilding at Lady St Mary, but pictures strongly suggest that the nave at least was Anglo-Saxon, and the arches between the nave and the side aisles, and into the chancel, look very like those at the pre-Viking church at Brixworth in Northamptonshire.

Other churches may have been founded by wealthy land-owners; that is the implication of Beaminster's name, recorded as *Bebingmynstre*, 'the church associated with a woman called Bebbe', or Yetminster 'the church of a man called Eata'. Churches founded

This fragment of sculpture in Gillingham was probably from a cross-shaft, and is carved with a complex knot of 'double-strand' interlace; the under-and-over effect is quite well done, and the pattern was probably cut from a prepared template – possibly the same one as was used for the similar panel on the East Stour cross (see page 65).

by the laity may have depended too much upon a particular family for long-term stability; Beaminster passed into the ownership of Gloucester Abbey by the end of the eighth century, and Yetminster had been acquired by Sherborne by the middle of the ninth.

The 'minster' in these names derives ultimately from the Latin *monasterium*, and was often used of large and important churches; Wimborne Minster is an example. Iwerne Minster takes its name from the local river, as do Sturminster ('Marshall' and 'Newton' were added much later) and Charminster, even though it is not until the eleventh century that the last name is recorded. In a few cases the name merely means that an estate was owned by a 'minster', not that there was an important church there: Lytchett Minster is an example. Names are not the only evidence of 'minster' status. Gillingham may have had an early 'minster' associated with the little-understood early cemetery there; the ninth century sculpture fragments also suggest an important church, as does its later donation by William I to the abbess of Shaftesbury in return for the castle hill at Corfe.

'Minsters' are sometimes referred to as 'mother-churches' because they originally had large parishes, usually subdivided later, though still bigger than average, with the result that they had bigger incomes, and could afford bigger buildings, right through the Middle Ages. There is a large church at Iwerne Minster, for instance, financed by its medieval parish, which was much bigger than those around it (and than it is to-day). It cannot be assumed that all 'minsters' are of the same early date, and in some cases their *parochiae* may be subdivisions of originally larger units, as Yetminster's might be of Sherborne's.

These 'mother-churches' provided a form of administration that brought a church physically closer to the people – partly for their spiritual needs, partly the better to ensure that they paid the taxes owed to the church on certain days of the year. Churches were expensive to run, and needed their estates to be efficiently managed, with reeves pressurized into producing more and more from their workforces and tenantries. Kings, too, were fully aware of the importance of efficient management, Ine's law-code setting out the produce owed to the king from every estate. Any new landlords would have been no more restrained by family ties than were the Church or the king from extracting as much as possible from those who worked the land.

That production increased in the later seventh century and later is strongly indicated by such discoveries as the water-mill constructed between 664 and 709 (such precision is possible because of tree-ring dating on surviving timber) at Worgret, outside Wareham, where a millstone suggests that grain was ground, and quantities of slag indicate that iron was being smelted, the wheel of the mill being used to raise hammers to crush the ore, and to power bellows for a furnace. There was both grain processing and iron-smelting near Gillingham; slag and what was probably a grain-drying oven were found underlying Christchurch's defences, which are attributable to the ninth century; and slag has been found at Wimborne. All these sites are on land which at one time or another in the Saxon period was owned by the Church or the king. Another sign of the importance of estate organisation is the acquisition by Sherborne in 774 of a piece of land at Lyme where salt was produced, needed in quantity to preserve food, and 'Domesday Book' shows how other churches also had coastal salt-houses.

Changes like these cannot always be closely dated, and there are others which may go with them that are only visible as very general trends. Increased production implies rising population, but it is still hard to find where people were living; pottery remains scarce, and without it the settlement sites remain almost impossible to locate, unless revealed by chance as at Alington Avenue. The way that the charters deal with land units may be significant; seventh and eighth century Dorset estates in the 'Sherborne Cartulary' were named topographically, such as *iuxta pedrian* ('by the River Parrott') and *in lydene* ('in the Lidden valley'), but by the ninth century they were known by the names of places, such as Bradford and Halstock, a change suggesting that by then people were thinking more in terms of specific site than of area, as though they had a more precise way of viewing the landscape and its resources. It also suggests that these places, many of them *tuns* and *worths,* were becoming fixed points, with shifting of occupation site becoming less likely to happen.

Perhaps allied to this increasing sense of precision was the re-arrangement of fields into long, narrow strips. King Ine's late seventh century law may be referring to something like this system when it talks of farmers having 'common meadow or other land divided in shares to fence, and some have fenced their portion and some have not', the latter owing compensation if stock broke in.

The timber foundations of what was probably an early eighth century mill
survived outside Wareham because they were below water-level and had not
rotted away from the usual process of getting wet, then dry, then wet again.
The slots in the substantial horizontal timbers were for upright posts;
the round stumps are the remains of piles driven into the mud to
try to stabilise the building above.

Quite what this means is not clear – medieval open-field strips were
not usually fenced, but the reference may be to temporary hurdling –
but it suggests firstly that there were fields divided into separate
holdings, and secondly that (unsurprisingly) frequent disputes arose
between neighbours because a new system involved new rights and
responsibilities. One royal estate that may have been replanned in
this way is Fordington, where the medieval parish all but surrounded
Dorchester, and probably shows the size of the estate; by the ninth
century, kings were signing charters at Dorchester, so they presumably had a residence, and land to go with it, somewhere near-by;
this would almost certainly have included Fordington. Between
Dorchester and Maiden Castle, fields divided into long, narrow strips
had survived largely intact from the Middle Ages when they were
mapped in 1779. They overlay and bore no relation either to the

pattern of Iron Age and Roman fields discerned from air photographs or to the post-Roman sites at St George's or Alington Avenue. The mid Saxon period may have seen the origins of many strip-field systems like those outside Dorchester.

Another change that came about slowly was the re-emergence of money. Two gold coins of the seventh century have been reported from Dorset, one from Weymouth probably having been set in a mount and worn as a valuable ornament, rather than used for currency. Early in the eighth century, silver coins now known as 'sceattas' began to circulate. Dorset is outside the area where they are most common, though a small cluster near Hod Hill may mean that there was a fair there, to which came merchants who were beginning to use money in their dealings. 'Sceattas' probably minted at Southampton imply that the shire was being drawn into the international commercial system in which that port had become prominent. Some of the reports of finds are not very reliable, so the amount of coin circulation in eighth century Dorset is difficult to gauge. As taxation and Church payments were increasingly demanded in cash rather than kind, however, more and more people would have had to acquire coin by selling their produce at a market, to meet their obligations. This transition was a slow process, and none of the places that were towns and market-places in later medieval Dorset can definitely be said to have been a trading-place in the mid Saxon period. Places where commerce might most be expected are the major Church or royal centres. Wimborne, Wareham and Sherborne all have towns where some parts look as though they were carefully laid out, with a wide street or small square for a market-place; these plans did not just grow piece-meal, but they are not really datable.

Dorchester has a plan based on the gates in the old Roman walls, though its main streets have deviated from the Roman lines, and the side streets seem to bear no relation to the Roman ones at all. Two pins with distinctive spiral heads are probably seventh or eighth century and a fine gold ring is probably late eighth or early ninth century, but they do not necessarily relate to any sort of urban life – they could have been dropped by someone visiting the king's residence, if that was inside the walls rather than in Fordington. Nevertheless, it may have been from Dorchester that the king's reeve

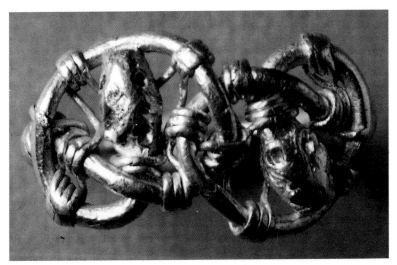

This gold ring, now in the Ashmolean Museum in Oxford, came from Dorchester, but no details about how and where it was found were recorded. It is made from a gold wire, interlaced at the front and ending in snakes' heads. A finer strand of gold wire is knotted in-between.
The ring is shown at about four times actual size.

set out in Brihtric's reign (786-802) to accost overseas visitors at Portland, who were later said to be the first Vikings; his interest was probably to ensure that they paid toll on any goods that they were bringing. Whatever, it cost the reeve his life.

THE FIRST VIKINGS

Despite the early skirmish at Portland, Dorset was too far round the coast to bear the main brunt of the Viking raids. No more attacks are mentioned until 840, when the Vikings were again victorious at Portland. The 'Anglo-Saxon Chronicle' says that 'the people of Dorset' were led by an *ealdorman*, the 'shire-reeve'. He had raised a troop from those who owed military service for their land, not a very effective force unless it had a backbone of well-trained members of the king's household. 'Dorset' is referred to here for the first time, and the levying of a troop from it shows that it was an administrative unit. It may have been composed of smaller districts, the hundreds, that are first recorded in the tenth century, but which probably have a much earlier origin.

The organisational structure of the ninth century was not enough to guarantee success against the Vikings, and King Alfred nearly succumbed. One of the lowest points of his reign was in 876 when 'the enemy army slipped past the army of the West Saxons into Wareham'. In the following spring, the Vikings left Wareham for Exeter, but their ships ran into a storm off Swanage, and a number (though perhaps not as many as the 120 stated by the 'Chronicle') were lost. Weakened, they did not return from Exeter to attack from the west, which may have been the original plan. At any rate, Dorset is not said to have been raided again in the ninth century.

The Vikings were not acting randomly. King Brihtric had probably been buried in its church because Wareham was a royal estate centre as well as having a religious community. It was a place well supplied with the taxation tribute owed from the country round, and stocks of food were a considerable attraction to Vikings needing somewhere to spend the winter. South-east Dorset contained a large amount of royal land, on which the king depended for men and supplies; capturing Wareham challenged his authority, at a time when other

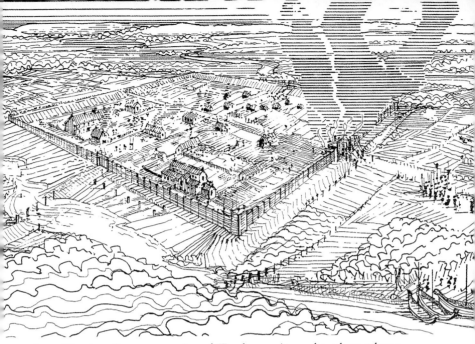

Peter Woodward's reconstruction of Wareham as it may have been when a defended place in the ninth century, with the River Frome in the foreground down which boats sailed out into Poole Harbour. The scale of some of the buildings inside, like Lady St Mary Church, has been exaggerated to allow more detail to be shown, though how many others stood inside the enclosure is unknown. The earth bank and the ditch in front of it can still be seen around much of the present town, and excavations justify the reconstruction of the timberwork. More problematical is the large building placed in the area where the castle was later built; a royal palace almost certainly existed somewhere in the immediate area, though not necessarily inside the 'burh'. The year is 876, and a Viking army is attacking the east gate, which they have set alight. Their boats have been pulled up onto the river-bank, as stakes have been driven into the water to stop them getting further upstream . . . Soon they will break in and set up their base for the winter.

Viking armies were taking control of whole kingdoms, and settling. The same fate threatened Wessex, and the 'Chronicle's' assertion that the Vikings gave Alfred hostages and swore him oaths on their holy ring (probably associated with Woden worship) cannot disguise his failure to stop them taking a strong-point from which he could not then dislodge them.

A recent attack on the authenticity of the 'Life' of Alfred purporting

The hill-top position of Shaftesbury is clearly seen in this photograph. On the right, the elegant broad walk cuts across the south side of the medieval abbey church, laid out in the lawns, with the nineteenth century Holy Trinity Church to the left. Beyond, the triangular market-place can be seen. Late Saxon pottery from the site of St Peter's Church shows how the town grew up around this area, outside the defences, with Gold Street, spilling down the hill to the right, a twelfth/thirteenth century extension.

to have been written by Asser, a churchman in the king's entourage, casts doubt on whether the Wareham church was a nunnery, since no other source gives this information, until an abbess is mentioned in the tenth century. In fact, the detail which Asser gives about the names of the rivers on either side of Wareham, and about its strong position, suggests local knowledge unlikely in a later forger. Consequently, Asser's description of Wareham as a *castellum* is probably a reliable statement that the place was fortified; not a 'castle' in the modern sense of a defended residence, but a place with earth banks and ditches, which still survive, particularly impressively on the west side, where the peninsula gives a dry-land route to Dorchester. Excavations have shown that the earth bank originally had a timber rampart along the top, later replaced by a stone wall.

A complex series of documents now known collectively as the 'Burghal Hidage' lists three places that were fortresses in late ninth/early tenth century Dorset – modern Dorset includes a fourth, Christchurch, then in Hampshire and known as 'Twynham'. These 'burhs' formed a chain of strong-points to deny the Vikings access to Wessex, and to provide a refuge for local people. Each had a number of hides 'belonging' to it, each hide having to supply one man, with four men needed to maintain each pole (16½ feet) of wall. Wareham had 1,600 hides 'belonging' to it; its banks go round three sides of the medieval town and measure about 2,180 yards, very close to the length that can be computed by multiplying 1600 by 16.5, and dividing it by four (and again by three to turn feet to yards). This resulted from careful measurement – a similar equation for Winchester is precise to one per cent.

For Shaftesbury, a wall length of 963 yards would be predicted from the 'Burghal Hidage'. No bank or ditch is visible to-day, but it would be expected to stretch across the steep-sided peninsula chosen by King Alfred as the site of a nunnery for his daughter, which Asser says was near Shaftesbury's east gate. Assuming that Alfred's church underlies the later abbey, and that it would have been inside the protection of the defences, a line from Tout Hill to Gold Hill looks likely, with the market-place outside a central gate. A parish boundary favours a line slightly west, however, and there are other possibilities.

The third Dorset 'burh' was *Brydian*. This could refer to a hillfort overlooking the Bride valley, but Bridport is most people's choice. The 'Burghal Hidage' would give a wall length of 1045 yards, which like the Shaftesbury figure suggests something long enough to cut off a promontory, but not enough to surround a settlement of any size. The curving line formed by Gundry and Folly Mill Lanes looks inviting, but traces of a bank further north may be a better candidate. This would put the present-day market, in the wide east-west street, outside the defences, with another perhaps inside where South Street widens out by the church.

Almost as interesting as the places included in the 'Burghal Hidage' are those excluded from it; why not Dorchester, with its Roman walls? why not Sherborne, and the bishop's cathedral? A coastal location was a primary consideration, with inland Shaftesbury perhaps chosen because of Alfred's personal concern. But in that case, why not somewhere near Weymouth, to protect the Dorchester area? The document raises many questions, but it does show that there was a systematic defensive strategy, and a means of allocating responsibility that would guarantee that the system was maintained. The allotment of exact numbers of hides, and the accuracy of lay-out at Wareham, suggests a precision which some would see as typical of King Alfred himself. Certainly the careful administration of the kingdom is revealed.

The provision for the 'burhs' also indicates considerable manpower resources and the ability to feed the men who were on their fortress duties. This strain on the local economy may have held back developments such as the growth of markets and towns. Dorset's three 'burhs' all went on to become towns in the following centuries, but it is difficult to judge how far this was the intention when they were set up. Churches like Wimborne and Wareham suggest mid Saxon prosperity, not entirely lost because of the Vikings; a sculpture at Cranborne is almost certainly late ninth century, for instance, as is the Bowleaze Cove jewel. A gilt mount from just outside Wareham is another object of the period, quite probably an import from Francia. There are no more ninth century 'pennies' from Dorset than of the eighth century 'sceattas', but that is a pattern across the whole country, and may not mean that the use of money was not increasing,

A small piece of sculpture at Cranborne is almost the earliest evidence for a church there. The animal has a strand of interlace passing through its body, a feature that dates it to the late ninth century. The piece may have been one of the arms of a cross, in which case the animal may have been the Bull, symbol of St Luke, flanking Christ on the Crucifix, with the Eagle of St John, the Man of St Matthew and the Lion of St Mark on the other three arms.

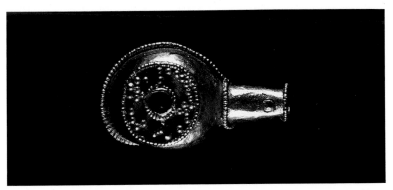

Calling this object the 'Bowleaze Cove jewel' disguises our ignorance of its function. Illustrated here at twice actual size, it is made of gold, and has a short open nozzle which probably held a short rod, of ivory or wood which has rotted away. Like the famous Alfred Jewel, its nozzle is not set centrally, but is in line with the back, as though to rest on a flat surface, such as the page of a book. It may have been an aid to a reader, for use to point to the word in a text. King Alfred's attempts to bring education to his kingdom was fostered by gifts of books and valuables to his churches.

Recently discovered in a garden just outside the defences
of Wareham, this silver mount had a thin coating of gold
to make it sparkle when it caught the light. The decoration
is of acanthus leaves, and it may well have been made on
the Continent and brought to England on a harness belt –
the lug on its back suggests that it was fastened to
something leather, rather than nailed to a box or casket.
shown here at about twice actual size.

only that the 'pennies' were larger and less likely to be lost. Stray
finds near Bere Regis suggest that the Dorchester-Badbury Roman
road was being used by traders, and a small hoard found near
Winterborne Whitechurch may have been hidden by someone rightly
worried about their future during the worst of the Viking raids.

THE LATE SAXON CHURCH

Dorset's various churches had mixed fortunes in the tenth and eleventh centuries. King Alfred's foundation at Shaftesbury continued to receive gifts of land from the Wessex royal family; a queen buried there in 944 came to be regarded as a saint. She was soon outshone by Edward the Martyr, murdered at Corfe in 978, and removed to Shaftesbury from Wareham the following year by Dorset's ealdorman. Edward rapidly became a cult figure, not for the holiness of his life, but for the manner of his death – princes who died young often became venerated, and Edward's murder was followed so quickly by the first of the renewed Viking raids that divine retribution seemed to have been brought down. Shaftesbury acquired a large estate centred on Corfe at some time after the murder, perhaps given by the king in expiation.

There are confused accounts of the discovery of a body that might be Edward's at Shaftesbury, and a glass bowl, now kept in Winchester Cathedral, might be a donation to his shrine. In June 1001, his coffin was translated from its original resting-place to the main altar. Yet in the same year, there were plans to move it, with the whole Shaftesbury community, to a more secure site at Bradford-on-Avon (Wiltshire), where the church built to receive the saint survives largely intact. This upheaval seems never to have taken place.

Dorset's earlier nunneries fared badly. When King Alfred died in 899, his nephew seized not only a royal residence at Wimborne and the fortress at nearby *Twynham* (Christchurch), but also a nun, as a way of claiming proprietorial rights over the church and challenging his cousin Edward's authority. No more is heard of Wimborne as a nunnery, though it survived as a church. In 962, a 'King Sigeferth killed himself, and his body is buried at Wimborne'; his is a Scandinavian name, and he was not a member of the Wessex royal house. He may have been a hostage from Dublin, Man or the Isles.

Wimborne was also included in a list of places where saints' bodies rested. The last mention of a nunnery at Wareham concerns the death of an abbess in 982. There was also a nunnery at Horton in the late tenth/early eleventh centuries. In the tenth century, there are several references to 'religious women' with estates, some of whom may have been widows living in seclusion with a few companions and servants; their houses were never intended to become formal communities, but entering a nunnery was not the only option for such ladies.

Despite ceasing to be nunneries, Wareham and Wimborne survived as 'mother-churches' for male priests, and new ones such as Canford, not heard of before the eleventh century, may have been founded to make the size of older minster *parochiae* more manageable, augmenting the system already probably operated from Yetminster, Beaminster and others. Even the bishopric was subject to reorganisation, Sherborne losing its authority over Wiltshire, Somerset and Devon in 909.

These were not the only ecclesiastical changes. King Alfred's grandson King Athelstan, a noted Church benefactor, founded a monastery at Milton in 933. A period of Reform that sought to reinforce the Benedictine ideal of a monastic, communal life involving no parochial duties was one reason for the foundation of Cerne Abbey in the 980s. In 998, Bishop Wulfsige refounded the chapter attached to the cathedral at Sherborne as a Benedictine house. Abbotsbury Abbey was established in the 1030s or later, and Horton was refounded as a male house, but was not endowed with enough land to be successful, and later merged with Sherborne. The church at Cranborne had quite large estates at the end of the eleventh century, and became a priory, but the late ninth century sculpture there is evidence of earlier importance.

No pre-Conquest buildings survive at the major churches, though the west wall and part of the north porticus at Sherborne, allied to evidence from excavations and a depiction on an eleventh century seal, show that even an impoverished bishopric could support quite a grandiose cathedral. At Wimborne, part of a north porticus survives encased in the twelfth century rebuilding, and the earlier church at Lady St Mary, Wareham, remained, there being no need to

The Saxon Cathedral of Sherborne c. 1050 JHPG 1969.

J.H.P. Gibb's reconstruction of the late Saxon cathedral at Sherborne is based partly upon surviving masonry at the west end and on the north side, partly on excavations, and partly on Sherborne's eleventh century seal. Like many important churches of the period, a grand west end provided not just a formal entrance, but in the upper tiers space for altars, and perhaps the bishop's throne. The main altar was probably in the east end of the nave, with the area under the crossing tower used by the priests during services. The east end and the side annexes were for lesser altars, burials, and the display of relics.

reconstruct it for its reduced role as a 'mother-church'.

Another development was subdivision of the 'mother-church' *parochiae* into smaller parishes, usually instigated by landlords from a mixture of piety and profit – a benefit to their tenants and themselves, as they had less far to travel to a church which could be maintained, and a priest for it paid, from tithes, burial fees and so on, with the possibility of a modest surplus. Christchurch had a *parochia* that covered much of the New Forest, but documents show how it was being broken up into smaller units both before and after the Conquest, a piece-meal process that was probably taking place widely – certainly 'Domesday' records a number of rural churches throughout Dorset. There were also parish divisions in towns. As

An eighteenth century engraving of St Martin's, Wareham, with the south side falling into picturesque ruin. The cottage obscures most of the late Saxon or early Norman chancel, but the tall and narrow proportions of the nave are a clue to its early origins. The tower, and the west end of the nave, were added after the Reformation.

East Gable

The north side of the chancel of St Martin's still has a small 'double-splayed' window. This nineteenth century drawing shows the 'long-and-short' work in the corners, and how the twelfth century north aisle abuts the earlier work.

well as Lady St Mary, Wareham had a church at each of its three gates, probably to encourage travellers to say a prayer and make an offering for a safe journey, and a fourth in the centre, as though to bless the market-place.

Many of the parish churches would have begun as wooden

The early tenth century East Stour cross-shaft is a magnificent sculpture with panels showing various plant and interlace patterns (see front cover).

The font at Melbury Bubb is an Anglo-Saxon cross-shaft, turned upside
down. It is carved with a series of animals that are taken from the
illustrations in 'Bestiary' books, some scarcely recognisable, like the hyena in
the photograph. It is shown eating a small dog, lured to it because the hyena
was said to imitate a human voice. The drawing shows the complete carving
the right way up, with the top of the font now at the bottom. In the centre,
a lion brings its cub to life by licking it, while the lioness looks on. On the
right, the stag is sucking the venom from a serpent. These themes all had
Christian allusions – the lion, for instance, takes three days to bring its cub to
life, just as Christ spent three days in a state of death before the Resurrection.

The Winterbourne Steepleton angel was probably part of a large Crucifixion scene, carved in the late tenth or early eleventh century. Its most likely original setting was high above the chancel arch, and it would have been painted, not bare stone.

buildings, later rebuilt in stone. Only Winterbourne Steepleton and Wareham St Martin have what might be pre-Conquest walls, though both may have been built by masons trained in Anglo-Saxon methods, but working for Norman lords. Wareham St Martin has an early type of window, long-and-short corner stones, and a plan that largely conforms to the same unit of measurement as had been used to lay out the defences, the Old English rod. But its complex chancel-arch, and the wall-painting in its chancel, would better fit a date of about 1100 than 1050; nevertheless, it is probably the earliest reasonably complete urban parish church in England.

The other physical evidence of a pre-Conquest church is an occasional piece of sculpture. Part of a fine early tenth century cross-shaft was found at East Stour, Winterbourne Steepleton has an angel which was probably part of a Crucifixion or other New Testament scene carved in the late tenth or early eleventh century, Stinsford has another, and there is an eleventh century cross-shaft now serving as Melbury Bubb's font. For a county so rich in building-stone, the total is rather meagre, suggesting that Dorset estate-owners had less money to spare than contemporaries elsewhere.

VIKINGS AND NORMANS

The relative peace of southern England in the first three quarters of the tenth century was shattered by renewed Viking attacks. Their ships were even bigger and stronger than before, so Dorset was much less immune from raids simply because of its distance from Denmark. Three merely ravaged Portland in 982, but in 994 a fleet took over Poole Harbour and 'went inland everywhere into Dorset as widely as they pleased'. By 1001, inland Shaftesbury was being considered an unsafe place for the nunnery, despite the defensible *burh* there.

Although Dorset was not listed as among the shires 'overrun' by the Vikings in 1011, it suffered again in 1015, when Cnut was in Poole Harbour. How much actual destruction all this means is unclear. A large army can do a lot of damage if it wants to – but a well-disciplined one may gain more from forcing people to pay tribute, and, by not burning the seed-corn, can come back for more another year. Probably just as bad was the English King Ethelred's need for heavy taxes to pay for his army and to buy off the Danes; that a bishop of Sherborne left money in his will to relieve his people of the burden of paying for ships shows the sort of pressures they were under.

The raids have not left a physical record in burnt churches and abandoned villages. Stone walls may have been added to the defences at Wareham and Christchurch at this period, but the dating is not secure. A fine sword with an antler handle found in the river at Wareham need not have been lost in action, but might have been dropped accidentally, or thrown in either as a sacrifice, or as a ritual to prevent its use after its owner's death. Around the year 1000, a hoard of sixty-five silver pennies was buried outside Shaftesbury, perhaps by someone fearful of a Viking raid, but more likely by a merchant reluctant to take so much money into the town, for fear of cut-purses; most of the coins were minted in London or in northern England, which suggests that they had been brought by a visitor, as a

The fronts and backs of some of the coins from the Shaftesbury hoard (or possibly hoards, as the coins were found at different times). All are silver pennies, with the design on the back giving them their name, the 'Long Cross' type, minted between about 997 and 1003. On the front is a bust of the king, with his name, Aethelred, and on the back the inscriptions give the names of the moneyers and the mints where they worked.

locally-assembled hoard would be expected to have more locally-minted coins in it.

The Danish Cnut's eventual success probably led to many confiscations so that the new king could reward his followers, Scandinavians such as Orc and his wife Tola, who received several estates, 'Agemund' (probably Aghmund) given land at Cheselbourne, and Bovi, of Horton. There were not many such immigrants, however, as they had no effect upon the language; very few Scandinavian personal names were recorded in Dorset in 'Domesday', and no place-names. Orc and Tola founded Abbotsbury Abbey, much in the way that an English aristocrat of the previous generation had founded Cerne; Bovi may have refounded Horton as an abbey; and Agemund is known because his estate passed to Sherborne, possibly by his own gift. It is as if these incomers were integrating themselves into Anglo-Saxon society by patronising the Church. Orc and Bovi were both referred to as Cnut's *ministri*, a Latin synonym for the English 'thegn', but were also both known by the Danish title, 'housecarl', as though the terms were interchangeable. In 1066, 'Domesday' records that Dorset's four towns were paying levies for the housecarls' service, so the word was still in use even after the end of the Scandinavian dynasty.

Cnut himself died at Shaftesbury, but his body was taken to Winchester to rest with those of earlier, English, kings. It would have been appropriate enough for him to have been left to lie with Edward the Martyr, and his removal may be a sign that Shaftesbury Abbey was not as influential as it had been. It was the second wealthiest nunnery in England in 1066, but even so it had had four of its estates seized by Earl Harold Godwin, who had ignored King Edward the Confessor's instruction to return them. If a Shaftesbury could not protect itself from secular predators, it was much worse for less well-connected churches. The nunnery at Wareham could not prevent the removal of the Martyr's potentially profitable body in 979, so presumably lacked important friends. It could have been destroyed dramatically in a Viking raid, but is as likely to have had to disband because it could not resist English or Danish lords who used their muscle-power to take over its estates.

No excavation in Dorset has revealed the houses of these pre-Conquest aristocrats, though examples elsewhere were built on quite a generous scale, with a variety of buildings within a compound that might have been surrounded by a ditch and bank, but which was not heavily fortified. Only at Corfe may anything survive; part of a fairly substantial first-floor stone hall standing on ground-floor storage space may already have been part of the royal residence when Edward was on his way to stay there, unless it was built later by an abbess of Shaftesbury. It may be King William's work, however.

The Normans caused even greater upset than the Danes to secular estate-owners, who were systematically dispossessed, except for a few of the least significant. These newcomers made no attempt to integrate; they founded no abbeys in Dorset, but instead patronised the churches in their homelands. King William gave Wareham church to St Wandrille, an abbey in Normandy, so that the benefit of its tithe and other income went overseas, and Queen Matilda gave land at Frampton to an abbey at Caen. Hugh fitzGrip, the first Norman

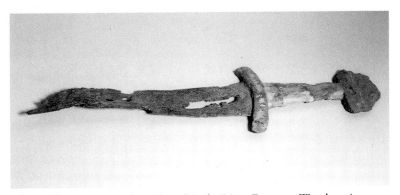

This tenth century sword was found in the River Frome at Wareham in 1927. The handle grip survives between the two guards and is made of horn, onto which was inscribed the owner's name. It began 'Aethel . . .', a name element only used by the royal family and aristocracy.

sheriff, deprived Abbotsbury of its dues from land at Waddon, transferring them to Montivilliers. The English churches retained most of their estates, though Sherborne, Glastonbury and Cerne suffered some loss. Only Cranborne seems to have received favour, gaining a small estate from Hugh fitzGrip.

'Domesday' shows that a few estates were less valuable in 1086 than they had been in 1066, and might not have recovered from ravaging soon after the Conquest, carried out as punishment for a revolt in the south-west centred on Exeter. On the whole, though, the changes probably reflect reorganisation and revaluing; some decreases may be apparent, not real, resulting from estate subdivisions. Dorset's four towns suffered badly in the twenty years after 1066, with half or more of their houses lost or destroyed. Although houses were often removed to allow castles to be built in major towns, in Dorset this is only certainly true for Wareham, where a castle is mentioned in 'Domesday'. It would not have been so large as to account for the destruction of all the seventy-three houses lost there after 1066, however. Dorchester's castle might be eleventh century, but is not recorded until later. Corfe is the only other castle in Dorset certainly begun by 1100, King William taking its site from the abbess of Shaftesbury in return for the church at Gillingham in what looks like an uncharacteristically fair exchange.

THE LAND AND THE TOWNS

'Domesday Book' is not a complete census; it is a record of who owned land in about 1086, and who had owned it in 1066, of what an estate should have been worth, and of what resources it had. As resources included people, there are statements about the number of peasants on an estate, but not the size of their families. Nor does it record all the free tenants, whose rents were part of an estate's value, but who were not a 'resource' at their landlord's disposal. Other problems include some estates not paying the normal taxes, for instance if a church had been given a favourable exemption by the king. Slightly under 7,500 country people are recorded. If each of them supported a family of five, at least 37,000 people were living in rural Dorset, but the true figure may have been quite a lot higher.

For a few estates, 'Domesday' reveals how many cattle, sheep and other stock the owner had on the home farm. Estates on Portland and parts of the Chalk were taxed very highly, with the rest of the county in the middle bracket, except for the heathland around Poole Harbour. The richest estates were those with the most sheep; the king had 900 on the 'island' of Portland, 1,600 at Puddletown. Most other owners' animals are not recorded, but very large flocks were clearly being kept. 'Domesday' does not say so, but the wool trade would have been the reason for this, not mutton or ewes' milk, though both had their value.

Other evidence about the economy of late Saxon Dorset comes from the land charters, which often include a list of the boundary markers because, in response to growing numbers of people to work the land more intensively, large estates were being divided up, and the new properties needed to be formally defined. Even if the boundary of a particular estate can be reconstructed from a charter – and there are often disagreements – reconstructing the estate pattern over a large area is difficult. Even more difficult is to know where people

Dennis Burden's reconstruction of some aspects of life in the late Saxon period. The woman and child gathering wood are a reminder that foraging was important, but the plough in the background was what kept most people fed. Thatch-roofed buildings with reasonably solid walls made with free-standing wooden posts, with the spaces between filled with daub, or daub-and-wattle, were probably the norm. A church, or at least a chapel, was increasingly likely to be found; in this picture, it has been shown as a plain building, because many were probably whitewashed, whether built of timber or of stone. It has a roof of wooden or stone tiles. This one had achieved parochial status, as the crosses show that it had a burial-ground.

actually lived. Although many of the places recorded in 'Domesday' can be assumed to have been grouped around the site of a church, many estates must have included scattered farms and hamlets, not separately recorded.

The backbone of the agricultural economy was the plough, pulled in some cases perhaps by no more than a single pair of oxen, but which may have been a team of eight on estates big enough to supply the necessary fodder. A long line of beasts needs a long turning-space, and so needs big fields. Occasional mentions such as that of an *ierthland* (= ploughland) or a *furh* (furlong) as boundary marks in charters show that in the tenth and eleventh centuries some estates were already extending their arable cultivation right up to the edges of their land. The open-field agricultural system that may have had pre-Viking origins, as at Fordington, was probably being further developed in the late Saxon period, and indeed on into the next centuries. Water-mills are recorded on most of Dorset's streams and rivers; even though their wheels could not produce much power, so that the numbers do not mean production of huge amounts of wheat (and barley for bran-bread in poor years) to be ground, there was quite enough being grown to justify the landlords' investment.

Large herds of cattle were needed to breed oxen for the plough, but cows were useful in their own right; many Dorset place-names contain *wick*, *wyke* or their equivalents, usually meaning dairy-farms. Milk could be turned into cheese for storage. Suitable parts of Dorset's coast-line, especially in Poole Harbour, were used for collecting and boiling salt, as a food preservative. Below modern Poole, huge quantities of oyster-shells show another way of exploiting the sea. Dorset had no industries such as iron-smelting recorded in 'Domesday', which includes but a single blacksmith – there must have been many others. Excavations show that pottery was being more commonly used in Dorset, but no kilns have been found. Some potters may have worked in the woods, as charcoal-burners would have done, moving around to where there was a suitable location to take loppings for another firing. Bowl-turners and barrel-makers were probably also exploiting the woods, of which Dorset had a fair amount, valuable also because pigs could be turned out in them. This was not wild wood, but a managed resource.

There must have been other craftspeople and traders, living and working in Dorset's towns, although the only ones of whom there is direct evidence are the moneyers, producing the silver pennies which were increasingly used during the tenth and eleventh centuries to pay rents and taxation. Consequently, farmers had to sell some of their produce and had to use the markets that the towns provided, to raise the necessary cash. Only four places in Dorset were normally licensed to have mints, Dorchester, Shaftesbury, Bridport and Wareham, all of which were active by about 930 – all but the first

Eleventh century aristocratic life is illustrated by these chess-pieces found at Witchampton. The piece with two heads is a bishop, the one-headed are knights, and the smallest is a pawn. Some of the pieces had been scorched, to blacken them.

had been named earlier, in the 'Burghal Hidage'. They were also the four places recognised as Dorset's towns by 'Domesday'. Several rural estates are recorded as owning houses in them, some probably for renting out, others as a base where the lord's reeve could arrange for some of the produce to be sold, and could buy what his lord required. There were such 'dependent houses' in Wimborne, implying a market there, even though it was not formally a borough. Markets were probably held at Sherborne, and perhaps at a few other places.

Excavations in Dorchester, Shaftesbury and Wareham have produced pottery and other artefacts that show how people were beginning to live in the towns in quite large numbers, though there is not much evidence about their streets or buildings. Small wattle-and-daub houses would not leave much trace in the ground, and they may have been no different from houses in the countryside. Only bigger towns had houses with cellars, for storage.

Shaftesbury in 1066 had the largest number of recorded *domus*, 257 – if a family of five lived in each *domus*, the population would have been around 1,300, but many people were probably not recorded because they were too poor to tax – as in Bridport, where 'twenty [of 120] are so run down that those who live in them are worthless for tax purposes.' *Domus* may mean 'a property', rather than an individual 'house'. The abbess had 151 burgesses in Shaftesbury, but only 111 habitable *domus*, so forty may have lived in sub-divided tenements. 'Domesday' does not record burgesses in the other towns, only *domus*, but that need not mean that none were sub-divided.

In Wareham, the king owned 143 *domus* in 1066, 'and now there are seventy', but 'in St Wandrille's part, there are 45 standing' – and the 1066 number is not given. 'The other barons', not identified, had '20 houses standing and 60 have been destroyed.' This figure may include the five owned by Horton Abbey, recorded elsewhere in 'Domesday'. None of the other three towns is stated to have had properties in them owned by anyone but the king or, in Shaftesbury, the abbess, but it is difficult to believe that only in Wareham were there other property-owners. So Dorchester may have had many more than the 172 houses recorded there in 1066, and Bridport more than 120, if only the king's were accounted for, other owners' town property being assessed as part of the income of one of their rural estates.

An estimate of the Domesday urban population is unlikely to be anything like accurate if there is so much under-recording. Even so, something well under 10,000 at 1066 is probable, and there were certainly substantial losses thereafter, even if many people remained in the towns, but became too poor to tax. As elsewhere in England, some townsfolk probably removed themselves to avoid the heavy taxation which made their businesses unviable. Presumably they disappeared among the rural poor.

By the end of the eleventh century, Dorset had become established as a county of middling wealth derived mostly from agriculture, with a few small towns, an important nunnery at Shaftesbury, and a major castle at Corfe. Britons, Saxons, Danes and Normans had all contributed to a basic framework that lasted in Dorset until the twentieth century.

FURTHER READING

Abbreviation: *PDNHAS – Proceedings of the Dorset Natural History and Archaeological Society*

Aston, M. and Lewis, C., eds, *The Medieval Landscape of Wessex*, Oxford, 1994

Bettey, J. H., *Dorset*, Newton Abbot, 1974

Coulstock, P. H., *The Collegiate Church of Wimborne Minster*, Woodbridge, 1993

Cox, P. W., 'A seventh century inhumation burial at Shepherd's Farm, Ulwell, near Swanage,' *PDNHAS*, 110 (1988)

Dark, K. R., *Civitas to Kingdom: British political continuity*, 300-800, Leicester, 1994

Davies, S. M., *et al.*, 'Excavations at Alington Avenue, Fordington, Dorchester, 1984/85: interim report', *PDNHAS*, 107 (1985)

Evison, V. I., 'The Anglo-Saxon finds from Hardown Hill', *PDNHAS*, 90 (1968)

Farwell, D. I. and Molleson, T. I., *Excavations at Poundbury. Volume 2: The cemeteries*, Dorset Natural History and Archaeological Society Monograph 11, 1993

Gelling, M., 'Why aren't we speaking Welsh?', *Anglo-Saxon Studies in Archaeology and History*, 6 (1993)

Hall, T., 'Witchampton: village origins', *PDNHAS*, 115 (1993)

Higham, N. J., *Rome, Britain and the Anglo-Saxons*, Manchester, 1992

Hill, D. and Rumble, A. R., eds, *The Defence of Wessex: The Burghal Hidage and Anglo-Saxon fortifications*, Manchester, 1996

Jarvis, K. S., *Excavations in Christchurch 1969-1980*, Dorset Natural History and Archaeological Society Monograph 5, 1983

Keen, L., 'The towns of Dorset', 203-48 in J. Haslam, ed., *Anglo-Saxon Towns in Southern England*, Chichester, 1984

Keen, L., 'An introduction to the Dorset Domesday', 1-26 in A. Williams and G. H. Martin, eds, *The Dorset Domesday*, London, 1991

Kelly, S. E., *Charters of Shaftesbury Abbey*, Oxford, 1996

Keynes, S., 'The lost cartulary of Abbotsbury', *Anglo-Saxon England*, 18 (1989)

Mills, A. D., *Dorset Place-Names; their origins and meanings*, Wimborne, 1986

Mills, A. D., *The Place-Names of Dorset*, English Place-Name Society Vol. 52, 1977 *et seqq.*

Murphy, E., 'Anglo-Saxon Abbey Shaftesbury – Bectun's base or Alfred's foundation?', *PDNHAS*, 113 (1991)

O'Donovan, M. A., ed., *The Charters of Sherborne*, Oxford, 1988

Penn, K. J., *Historic Towns in Dorset*, Dorset Natural History and Archaeological Society Monograph, 1, 1980

Royal Commission on Historical Monuments, *Dorset*, London, 1952-72

Smith, R. J. C., *et al.*, *Excavations along the Route of the Dorchester By-Pass, Dorset*, 1986-8, Wessex Archaeology Monograph 1, 1997

Sparey Green, C., *Exacavations at Poundbury. Volume* 1: The settlements, Dorset Natural History and Archaeological Society Monograph 7, 1987

Sparey-Green, C., 'Poundbury, Dorset: settlement and economy in late and post-Roman Dorchester', 121-52 in K. R. Dark, ed., *External Contacts and the Economy of late Roman and post-Roman Britain*, Woodbridge, 1996

Taylor, C., *Dorset*, London, 1970

Woodward, P. J., 'A comparison of coin groups from Romano-British settlements in Purbeck – a reflection of their contrasting status?', *PDNHAS*, 102 (1980), and *ibid.*, 103 (1981)

Woodward, P. J., Davies, S. M. and Graham, A. H., *Excavations at Old Methodist Chapel and Greyhound Yard, Dorchester*, 1981-84, Dorset Natural History and Archaeological Society Monograph 12, 1993

Yapp, W. B., 'The font at Melbury Bubb: an interpretation', *PDNHAS*, 111 (1989)

Yorke, B., *Wessex in the Early Middle Ages*, Leicester, 1995

ACKNOWLEDGEMENTS

The names of many of those I would to thank for their help are contained either in the Further Reading or the illustration acknowledgements below. But as the publication of this book falls within the twenty-fifth year of my involvement with Dorset's archaeology, it seems an appropriate moment to place on record my gratitude to Lilian Ladle of Wareham for her support, interest and encouragement throughout the whole of that time.

I would particularly like to thank Peter Woodward, not only for his reconstruction of a Viking attack on Wareham on page 55, but also for his help with the photography of objects in Dorset County Museum. I am also grateful to Christopher Chaplin for the maps, and Dennis Burden for his reconstruction of Saxon village life on page 73, the drawings on pages 12 and 39, and the plan of Poundbury on page 32.

I am grateful to the following for allowing the inclusion of illustrations in their possession or for which they hold the copyright. The Ashmolean Museum, Oxford; page 53: British Museum (© British Museum); front cover, page 59 (bottom): Cambridge University Collection of Air Photographs; pages 17, 21: Dorset County Museum; pages 4, 28 (bottom), 29, 71, 75: J.H.P. Gibb; page 63: Hampshire County Council Museums Service; page 28 (top): W. S. Putnan; page 51: Royal Commission Historical Monuments (England), © Crown Copyright; pages 18, 26, 27, 37, 47, 48, 58, 59 (top), 65, 66: Wessex Archaeology; frontispiece, pages 24, 43.

The

DISCOVER DORSET

Series of Books

A series of paperback books providing informative illustrated
introductions to Dorset's history, culture and way of life.
The following titles have so far been published.

All the books about Dorset published by The Dovecote Press
are available in bookshops throughout the county,
or in case of difficulty direct from the publishers.
The Dovecote Press Ltd, Stanbridge,
Wimborne, Dorset BH21 4JD
Tel: 01258 840549   www.dovecotepress.com